BREAK THE MENTAL BARRIERS

CONQUER OBSTACLES, BUILD RESILIENCE, AND TURN SETBACKS INTO VICTORIES

KR GOSWAMI

Lata Gosai

This book is dedicated to Mrs. Lata Gosai,

the homemaker in Jamnagar (Gujarat), whose warmth, grace, and unwavering support have illuminated my journey with a nurturing spirit in creating a haven of love and harmony is truly inspiring.

Contents

Foreword

In a world pulsating with challenges and uncertainties, the journey toward personal triumph often feels like an arduous climb, laden with mental barriers that threaten to overshadow our potential. I want to offer you this book as a roadmap for those seeking to navigate the intricate terrain of their minds and emerge victorious on the other side.

There is a transformative expedition, where you will contour your limitations and you can redefine the whole process. Let your power of resilience be unearthed. I have no purpose for this book as a collection of motivational platitudes; it is a toolkit meticulously crafted to help you shatter the mental barriers that have held you back, and in doing so, unlock the latent potential that resides within.

It is now time to go through your intricacies of conquering obstacles, the narrative will unfold everything as a beacon of guidance, offering insights, practical strategies, and profound wisdom to empower you in your pursuit of personal excellence. The rest of the book will serve as a stepping stone, leading you through the labyrinth of challenges, teaching you not only to withstand adversity but to harness its energy to propel yourself forward.

Prepare to witness the metamorphosis of setbacks into victories, as the pages of this book unravel some of the stories which were confronted with mental barriers and emerged triumphant. It might be a testament to the human spirit's capacity to endure, adapt, and ultimately thrive in the face of adversity.

This book may be a call to action; it is an invitation to embark on a transformative but difficult journey, where the mind becomes a fertile ground for resilience to flourish, obstacles to crumble, and setbacks to metamorphose into the stepping stones of triumph.

As we discuss this expedition together, let the words within these pages be the catalyst for your revolution—a revolution that begins in the mind and echoes through every facet of your existence.

So, let us begin.

All the best!

KR Goswami

Author

Preface

Join Our Inner Circle!

Welcome to the journey of self-improvement and personal transformation. Con

gratulations on taking the first step towards becoming the best version of yourself. In this empowering journey, you'll discover the tools, strategies, and wisdom that will help you unlock your hidden potential, overcome obstacles, and achieve your dreams.

But this journey is not meant to be traveled alone. It's about joining hands and working together committing to growth and success. It's about forging a connection that will propel you to new heights.

By becoming a part of my exclusive association, you're not just getting value-added emails from me; you're joining a movement.

Here's what you can expect:

1. **Inspirational Insights: Receive weekly doses of motivation, wisdom, and inspiration that will fuel your drive to conquer your goals.**
2. **Exclusive Content: Gain access to bonus content, expert interviews, and sneak peeks into upcoming projects to stay ahead in your personal development journey.**
3. **Member-Only Offers: Enjoy special discounts, early access, and personalized recommendations that will accelerate your growth.**
4. **Supportive souls: Connect with expert individuals who share your passion for personal growth, providing a support system to help you overcome challenges and celebrate victories.**

If you are ready to elevate your life,

Click the link below to join in this transformative adventure with us. Your success story begins here, and we can't wait to be a part of it! Together, we'll build the best version of yourself.

https://krgoswami.com/join-hands.html

However, it is optional, your journey to greatness starts with this one click. Don't let this opportunity pass you by. You can seize it with unwavering determination!

Thank you for choosing to be part of our intellectual minds. Together, we will build a brighter, better future, one step at a time.

Lessons I Learned from My Life Events

As a working mother of a vibrant two-year-old, my journey has been a balancing act of responsibilities, aspirations, and the constant pursuit of overcoming mental barriers. Let me share insights gleaned from my own experiences. This is how I've navigated the intricate dance between work, motherhood, and personal growth.

For many working moms like myself, the challenge lies not just in managing the demands of a career, but also in equally nurturing and supporting our families. The mental barriers we face can sometimes feel overwhelming, as we juggle countless tasks and responsibilities on a day-to-day basis. However, I've discovered a few approaches that have helped me unwind and emerge stronger on the other side.

One of the most effective tactics I've employed is the power of distraction through work. While it may seem counterintuitive, immersing myself in tasks at the office has provided a much-needed respite from the chaos of home life. Focusing on work not only keeps my mind engaged but also allows me to channel my energy into something productive, giving me a sense of accomplishment and purpose that transcends any mental hurdles I may encounter.

In addition to staying focused on work, I've found solace in the soothing embrace of calming music. Whether it's the gentle melodies of classical compositions or the tranquil sounds of nature, listening to music has become an integral part of my daily routine. It helps me maintain a sense of calm and clarity amidst the busyness of the day, serving as a powerful tool for centering my thoughts and emotions.

Furthermore, I've learned the importance of starting my day early to ensure both my mind and work are fresh and sorted. Waking up before the rest of the world allows me to set the tone for the day ahead, carving out precious moments of quietude and reflection before the hustle and bustle begins. This early morning ritual has become a sacred time for me to center myself, align my priorities, and prepare for whatever challenges may lie ahead.

As I reflect on my journey as a working mother, I'm reminded of the resilience and determination that reside within each of us. Despite the obstacles we may face, we possess an innate ability to overcome adversity and emerge stronger on the other side. Some days are better than others and we always end up giving ourselves less credit to the person we have become! To say it out loud, I'm proud of the woman I have become!

Dear working mothers, embrace your unique journey and recognize the strength that lies within you. There is boundless potential that awaits you on the other side of every barrier and you are stronger than you give yourself credit for.

My heartfelt congratulations to KR Goswami on the successful crafting and publication of his title, 'Break the Mental Barriers.' Wishing him all the best on this remarkable achievement.

Shrinidhi T,

a certified content and copywriter from Dakshina Kannada, Karnataka, India

<u>LinkedIn</u> **Profile**

Voices of Resilience: Shared Journeys of Breakthroughs

Before we dive into the content, let's take a moment to acknowledge and appreciate the friends whose stories illuminate the path to overcoming mental barriers.

Meet the extraordinary individuals whose real-life experiences have woven into the fabric of this book, each contributing a unique thread to the tapestry of breaking mental barriers.

The Path to Mental Liberation

Even though our Indian society is regarded as being quite progressive, talking about our psychological boundaries can be challenging, particularly for a kid who is growing up. This isn't because adults lack the knowledge to mentor the next generation; rather, it's because people lost sight of their goals at some point, turning simple questions into in-depth inquiries and impairing our generation's ability to communicate.

I always considered myself to have been introverted, preferring solitude and quietness over noise. This quietness has shaped my perception and life journey, with some people loving me for my presence and calm demeanor, while others saw it as an opportunity to assert dominance. As a teenager, while girls my age were happy to be seen as social butterflies, I became a piece of furniture in the house or a fly on the wall at a party, preferring the solace of my own.

Some people have admired me for my silence, finding consolation in my presence and comfort in my peaceful demeanor. Others, however, viewed it as an opportunity to show their control, viewing me as an easy target to abuse and humiliate because I am different. But, despite this, no one bothered to probe deeper, to comprehend the reasons behind my silence.

Some took pleasure in my compliance, satisfied with having a family member who always followed instructions without question. Along the way, I lost sight of my aspirations, with the pursuit of a specific career fading into the background as I struggled to find my voice in a society that favored extroversion. This is when I once tore off my CA entrance exam application form, without discussing it with anyone in the family, when they went through a financial loss.

I studied extensively, relying on others for guidance in my education and career choices. I frequently switched jobs, accumulating diverse experiences but never truly mastering any field. Despite my efforts, I felt a sense of emptiness and a need for direction and longed for clarity on my desired career path, but amidst the uncertainty, I felt a sense of missing something.

In my mid-twenties, I constantly sought meaning and fulfillment in my life, seeking better learning and career advancement. I considered switching jobs and moving to a new city, but due to their family's orthodox beliefs, such a move was not feasible, leading to a prolonged period of familiarity in my life.

When I got engaged, everything changed. I believed that happiness had finally found me because of my partner's understanding and supporting character. Exploring a different culture allowed me to open up about my past, and my dreams. This period also allowed me to overcome barriers like trying meat for the first time or recording my voice for the role of Radio jockey or voice-over artist. Even with this newfound support, though, I still felt lost, even though there was a chance for a new beginning, I had lost interest in pursuing a job in favor of earning money alone.

For eight years, my career took a backseat as I embraced motherhood. However, the COVID-19 pandemic provided an opportunity to pause, stay home, and reconnect with loved ones. These challenging times tested my physical and mental health, pushing me to the brink of vulnerability and questioning my existence. Despite this, a ray of hope emerged when a friend reached out to me in despair, battling their mental demons.

Setting aside my struggles, I became their confidante, offering support and reassurance until they found solace once more. At that moment, I recalled the wisdom imparted by my mentor, reminding me of my own strength and resilience. "You are a powerful human being," he would say, "and you will understand your value when life presents you with its toughest challenges."

This was a big life-changing event for me. When I thought back on my previous interactions with friends, family, and neighbors, I realized that I was an empathic person who could listen intently without providing advice but would still lend a sympathetic ear. Open communication of emotions, in my opinion, is the first step toward resolving half of the issues.

This insight motivated me to start a new path as a counselor, filling a hole in my heart that I wanted to help others by just being a kind listener who doesn't pass judgment and walks with them on their path. I enrolled in a course to give myself the essential tools, and I started my adventure by getting involved with Unmukt

Bachpan, an NGO run by Mr Amit Batla, which allowed me to meet and talk to a variety of people. Though I joined in as a volunteer, Amit ji's journey to make a difference in other's lives and his battle with his own demons helped me stand up against mine.

Over the years, my interactions with children and the guidance of mental health professionals have been transformative. It was during this time I met Mr. Kantigiri Goswami, at a session, and his journey inspired me. As we discussed and shared ideas, I got to learn about his past experience within the Indian Airforce and what inspired him to become a motivational speaker. His capability to work on multiple projects sharing his stories allowed me to move out of my comfort zone and share mine with others. I utilized his methodology of sharing knowledge with personal examples, which led me to connect better with my audiences. Not only have these experiences helped me grow personally, but they have also shattered barriers, instilling in me the confidence to engage with new individuals without hesitation. I realized that surrounding myself with like-minded individuals fosters confidence and independence, a lesson I aim to impart to others.

Today, I stand as a proud mother and a confident partner, equipped to tackle challenges and make tough decisions, whether in my personal or professional life. I along with my husband founded Lakshya Saarthi, a platform for self-help and career guidance and have taken multiple successful workshops and webinars for both kids and adults, helping them communicate their minds. Lakshya Saarthi which literally means "the guide to your destination" allowed us to help individuals identify their goals and be soundboard to their ideas, mentoring them in achieving those goals. I successfully ran a project called "Red Ribbon " along with my team of young volunteers discussing emotional and physical changes people go through as a teenager. Currently I am working on a series of my podcasts discussing the importance of breaking boundaries.

We are available on lakshyasarthi.com and on social medias like Instagram and Facebook for all who would like to connect.

Mrs. Suman Khannah

Emotional Counsellor

New Delhi

My biggest failure in life and how could I overcome

I used to dream bigger from my childhood days. I was born and brought up in rural area which was one of the most backward districts of West Bengal at that time. I was more inclined to play and spend time with friends than to spare more time in studying like a brilliant scholar. Being a student of moderate intelligence, I could not score 1st division in my Higher Secondary Examination results. I had to contended with mere 53% score, when 1st division was 60% This was my biggest failure in life and I take responsibility of the same as I was not very careful examination. I used to perform much better in class texts, than those who scored 1st Division in the W B Board examination.

This was my biggest failure as I could not get admission in Engineering / Medical degree courses where minimum entry level requirement was 1st Division. Somehow, I could get admission in Bachelor of Science in a Christian College in our district town. After completing 3 years B.Sc. degree, I was trying hard for admission in M.Sc. but there also I failed as I did not score 1st class.

We were not very rich also financially and I had to search for jobs. From 1970 to 1973 I was relentlessly trying to get a job. The repeated failures in competitive examinations could not discourage me from trying further. I knew getting a good job was not easy but I did not quit trying. Ultimately, I succeeded in getting offer of employment in Central Security Force, Government of India, in 2nd half of 1973. Joining in early January 1974 in CSF, changed my life. It helped to gain physical as well as mental fitness and I again started taking up Post Graduate courses. I completed Membership Examination from IFE, Leicester, UK, which was equivalent to BE in Fire Engineering in India. I qualified MA (Economics), M.Sc. (Ecology & Environment), MBA (HR / Marketing Management). I embarked on a voyage of life ling learning. I completed Post Graduation and Ph.D. from Indian Institute of Technology, Kharagpur, the coveted institution across the world where getting admission is like going to heaven.

I changed service one after the other and employers were more interested to take me in their companies. The scenario was completely changed in 3 to 4 decades. During an educational trip being sponsored by IIT Kharagpur I went to USA for a short course in University of Nebraska at Omaha (UNO) where I got the chance to personally meet the most renowned American Businessman and Philanthropist Mr. Warren Buffet and had a lunch with him. I was very happy to be blessed by him and attending the course at UNO.

After serving over three decades in manufacturing and services sectors, I joined education sector and before starting writing books I was serving as Director, Post Graduate Studies, in SSRC, Bangalore, India.

I feel I could overcome the initial failures in my life by dint of hard labor, being resilient trying again and again and not quitting till I achieve my goals. To me dedication and perseverance are the keys to success and prosperity.

I have learned a lot from the writing of KR Goswami especially from his Ideal Version Series books. I wish him for his latest publication "Break the Mental Barriers"

Gurudas Bandyopadhyay, Ph.D.

Https://drgurudas.com

The Unseen Battles of My Life

In my life's narrative, I encountered the formidable challenge of depression on two separate occasions. The first instance unfolded when I experienced failure in my 12th-grade Science exams, which dealt a severe blow to my confidence. Subsequently, I withdrew from the outside world, confining myself to my room for a year, grappling with a profound sense of embarrassment. Despite these struggles, I summoned the resilience to attempt the exams again, eventually succeeding. It was during this tumultuous period that I sought solace in the wisdom found in mythological literature, such as the Bhagavad Gita, and other regional texts, which played a pivotal role in helping me overcome the initial phase of depression.

However, the journey was far from smooth, as I encountered another setback during my first year of B.Sc. graduation, plunging me into a second bout of depression. It was during this trying period that I forged a deep connection with Shetal, who later became my better half. Her unwavering support and encouragement became instrumental in my battle against depression. To sustain myself, I took up a part-time job as a gym trainer, eventually transitioning to a full-time position while pursuing my graduation.

The incorporation of regular exercise and structured routines not only transformed my lifestyle but also significantly enhanced my academic performance.

During the initial year of my B.Sc., I secured a mere 45% in my exams. However, with the consistent application of exercise principles and the unwavering support of Shetal, I managed to complete my B.Sc. with an impressive 71% and secured the 17th rank in the University. This reaffirmed my belief that regular physical activities, coupled with the support of loved ones, possess the capacity to dismantle mental barriers.

Embarking on my M.Sc. in Bioinformatics, I continued to harness the power of positive thinking, exercise, and a robust support system. This approach bore fruit, as I attained the remarkable feat of securing the 5th rank among 1500 students at Gujarat University. The challenges in my father's life further enriched my understanding and fueled my determination to rediscover my untapped potential. In essence, the amalgamation of positive mindset, physical activity, and a strong support network not only shattered mental barriers but also bestowed upon me newfound confidence and resilience.

KR Goswami, a dedicated fitness aficionado, consistently engages in rigorous workout sessions at the fitness center. Notably, he authored the outstanding book "Master Your Muscles." I am delighted to learn that he has ventured into a new realm with his latest title, "Break the Mental Barriers," focusing on mental toughness.

I extend my heartfelt best wishes to KR Goswami for his latest endeavor. May "Break the Mental Barriers" resonate with readers and contribute to their journey towards enhanced mental resilience.

Admin Director (Operations)

Zeus Fitness Centre

Ahmedabad

Metropolitan Dreams to Rural Triumphs

In the quaint town of Amreli, nestled between rolling farms and trees, I live as a young dreamer with my husband. I always believed that life was an endless journey of learning, an intricate tapestry woven with the threads of experiences.

My path led me through wider experiences in life, where my family helped me to achieve my dreams. I ventured deeper into the reading, exams along household work with delicate relationships with my in-laws.

I captured and played my role in a symphony of existence with multifaceted experience of work and life balance.

Each interaction whether at home or office was not that easy which I believed. Whether joyous or challenging, I became stronger and on my ongoing education simultaneously.

I immersed myself in studies along with the ebbs and flow of relationships, discovering the complexities of human emotions. Life is not just about weeping or shading tears during the inevitable circumstance. I realized that every connection, fleeting or lasting, added depth to my understanding of the human experience.

I embraced the unpredictability of life, understanding that challenges were not roadblocks but stepping stones toward growth. Each twist and turn in her journey became a classroom, and every experience was a teacher guiding her toward wisdom.

I was born and raised in a metropolitan city, fueled by dreams of achieving the extraordinary. Despite my initial lack of knowledge about competitive exams, I sought classes in Ahmedabad, only to find unsatisfactory results. Enter Ashish, my husband from the remote town of Amreli, Gujarat. Financial struggles persisted, but my passion for teaching prevailed. I coached 58 students, waiving fees for those in need.

Undeterred, I tackled the GPSC exam, passing on the first attempt. Currently holding a respected post, I refuse to settle. With upcoming exams, my aspiration reaches higher positions and designations shortly.

In the twilight of her adventure, I reflected on the profound truth I had discovered. Life, I realized, was a continuous process of learning from every new situation and event. The tapestry of my existence was a mosaic of lessons, each woven with threads of joy, sorrow, love, and resilience.

With a heart filled with gratitude and a mind enriched by experiences, I am ready to embrace the next chapter of my journey becoming a class II officer soon.

I'm delighted that my relative, KR Goswami, has contributed globally with 24 books and coached students for the National Defence Academy and banking careers. Proudly, I wish him success with his upcoming title, "Break the Mental Barriers."

Mrs. Sweta Gosai,

Executive Magistrate,

Amreli, Gujarat

My Mental Agony and Resolution

In the interconnected and varied elements of a situation of life, we find ourselves entangled in storms that threaten to dismantle the very essence of our being. It is amidst these tumultuous tempests that we unearth a reservoir of strength within, a strength necessary to endure the chaos that surrounds us. The pages you hold in your hands tell a story - my story - a narrative that unfolds in "Break the Mental Barriers" by KR Goswami. Within these lines lies a testament to resilience, a guiding light that emerges from the crucible of my own experiences and the stories of those who have confronted the darkest corners of existence.

I am BD Shingarakhia, a retired manager from one of the largest PSU banks, and I invite you to join me on this deeply personal journey. As a Sanyasi of Osho, I embarked on a spiritual odyssey, seeking refuge from life's harsh realities. Yet, even the shelter of spirituality couldn't shield me from the inevitable trials. The recent loss of my father, the weight of lifelong attachments, and the tempests that haunted me since childhood appeared as insurmountable challenges. However, my story takes an unexpected turn, revealing the transformative power of wisdom and resilience.

Immersed in the profound teachings of Osho, I faced a professional crisis that forced me to relinquish my managerial position. Serious allegations cast a foreboding shadow over my career, echoing the unpredictable twists that life can throw our way. Yet, the true test of my mettle came in the form of a selfless act—supporting a friend battling cancer, giving away all my possessions, and finding myself plunged into a financial abyss. Burdened by debts, I sought sanctuary in a new town, evading those seeking repayment.

One might anticipate defeat in the face of such adversity, but I found solace in the literature and discourses of Osho. My survival, against overwhelming odds, stands as a testament to the transformative power of knowledge and introspection. My journey mirrors the resilience of an elephant extricating itself from the challenging terrain, emerging gracefully from the metaphorical mud.

KR Goswami, a beacon of inspiration, played a pivotal role in helping me navigate these storms. His motivational writings and articles, showcased in his books, served as a guiding light, offering support during my darkest moments. My story serves as a powerful endorsement of the transformative potential inherent in breaking through mental barriers.

As you immerse yourself in the pages of "Break the Mental Barriers," let my journey inspire you to face your own challenges with courage and resilience. These are not mere narratives; they are beacons of hope, urging you to transcend limitations and discover the untapped strength that resides within you.

Wishing you a transformative and enlightening journey through these pages,

BD Shingarakhia
Manager, PSU bank (Retired)

Acknowledgements

I am sincerely grateful to the remarkable friends and cherished relatives who have made invaluable contributions to the narratives within my book through the sharing of their resilient and inspiring stories. Your generosity in imparting these experiences has enriched the pages and added depth to the themes explored. Thank you for being an integral part of this creative journey.

Heartfelt Appreciation to,

1. Dr Gurudas Bandyopadhyay
2. Mrs. Suman Khannah
3. Mr. Jay Acharya
4. Mrs. Shrinidhi T
5. Mrs. Sweta Gosai
6. Mr. BD Shingarakhia

Prologue

About The Author

The author boasts a commendable 15-year tenure of active service in the Indian Air Force, specializing in the meticulous maintenance and repair of Aero Engines across a diverse fleet of aircraft deployed in the Armed Forces. Focusing his expertise in technical trade, he honed his skills with a specialization in Helicopter and fighter aircraft engines. His service spanned various regions of the country, including the challenging terrains of Leh-Ladakh and Jammu and Kashmir, contributing to crucial operations such as Blue Star, Blast Track, Pawan and Passive Air Defense during peacetime. Not confined to Air Force Units alone, he extended his valuable services to the Army in Air Defense Regiments, demonstrating versatility in handling .303 rifles and LMGs alongside his aircraft-related responsibilities. As a supervisor, he assumed leadership roles overseeing specific security levels at different Air Force units.

Transitioning to a 24-year managerial role in the public sector banks and Reserve Bank of India, the author excelled in the supervisory cadre, undertaking diverse responsibilities as a field officer, cash officer, account officer, and branch manager across various branches in Gujarat. His outstanding contributions led to the recognition of several branches as 'Exceptionally Well Run,' aligning with the bank's high standards. Serving as a joint custodian of the Reserve Bank of India, he managed cash flow for ATM replenishments and Currency Administrative Cells of SBI and other banks. His remarkable achievements culminated in being honored as the Best Branch Manager of State Bank of India in the year 2014-15.

Academically, the author holds a master's degree in psychology, earned in 1986 from a prestigious university in South India. Throughout his service in the Armed Forces and the corporate sector, he applied his psychological insights to guide organizations and individuals, leveraging both experiments and experiences to address day-to-day challenges. Complementing this, he acquired computer skills, studying DISM and PGDCA from Saurashtra University and obtaining a degree from APTECH. In addition to his professional duties, he devoted spare time to teaching students MS Office, C++, Visual FoxPro, visual basics, and website designing.

Beyond his professional pursuits, the author is a multifaceted individual with a passion for vocal and instrumental music, showcasing his talents on instruments like the harmonium, guitar, flute, mouth organ, and violin. As an artist of All India Radio, he has performed numerous programs on both radio and stages across different parts of Gujarat. Presently, he is channeling his creative energy into various niches, including books and videos on banking, meditation, motivation, music, and diverse topics exploring human psychology, personality traits, and attitudinal effects on behavior. There are couple of dozens of books he has crafted for readers from all over the world.

Break the Mental Barriers
Conquer Obstacles, Build Resilience, and Turn Setbacks into
Victories

CHAPTER ONE

Mindset Mastery: The Power Within

In the vast landscape of personal development, the cornerstone of transformative change lies in the realm of the mind. I welcome you to this exclusive journey. It will serve as a gateway to profound self-discovery and empowerment. As we venture into the depths of this transformative exploration, prepare to embark on a journey that transcends the ordinary, where the canvas of your thoughts becomes the masterpiece of your life.

Take my words as affirmation. There is immense potential residing within you, waiting to be awakened and harnessed. "Mindset Mastery" is not just a concept; it is a dynamic force that shapes the lens through which you perceive the world, interpret challenges, and ultimately chart the course of your destiny. Let me try to unravel the intricacies of the mind, understanding its influence on our actions, decisions, and the unfolding narrative of our lives.

Navigate my friend through the corridors of mindset mastery, and uncover the keys to breaking free from self-imposed limitations and unleashing a reservoir of untapped power within. This journey goes beyond theoretical concepts; it is a practical guide infused with actionable strategies, real-life anecdotes, and transformative exercises that will empower you to reshape your mindset and, consequently, your reality.

The pursuit of mindset mastery is a profound undertaking, demanding self-reflection, courage, and a willingness to challenge ingrained beliefs. Whether you seek personal growth, professional success, or a more fulfilling life, the principles within this book will serve as a compass, guiding you toward a mindset capable of conquering obstacles and turning setbacks into stepping stones.

So, fasten your seatbelt and get ready to get on a voyage into the heart of your mind. It is an invitation to rediscover the extraordinary potential that resides within you, awaiting your acknowledgment and activation. As we navigate this transformative terrain together, prepare to witness the emergence of a mindset that transcends limitations, embraces possibilities, and lays the foundation for a life of resilience, purpose, and triumph.

The Mindset Mastery

Set the stage for the exploration of the mind's intricacies, inviting you to understand the pivotal role your mindset plays in shaping the course of your life. Discover the keys to unlocking a mindset capable of conquering obstacles and turning setbacks into triumphs. Let me narrate my real story.

In the early morning at 9 AM, I ascended the ladder of the helicopter to adjust the engine's RPM while the pilot initiated the engine run. Within the maintenance bay, a colleague had ingeniously secured a thread to a screwdriver and a spanner, ensuring their stability during the intricate task of aircraft maintenance. The optimal speed for the turbine engine stood at 33,500 RPM, allowing for variations of + and - 200 to ensure peak performance.

As I meticulously manipulated the RPM by adjusting the screw, the delicate balance between increasing and decreasing rotations unfolded. Unexpectedly, the thread, initially fastened to the tools for safety, was drawn into the air intake, taking the unfortunate spanner with it. The repercussions were immediate — the spanner fragmented, causing substantial damage to the aircraft engine and incurring a significant financial setback.

In a swift response, I leaped ten feet from the aircraft and urgently signalled the pilot to cease the engine's operation. Fortunately, he promptly complied. However, the speed of events escalated, and within a mere 15 minutes, Air Force police descended upon the scene, detaining me for subsequent inquiry. The mental stress in that moment was palpable, leaving an indelible mark on the gravity of the situation.

As your curiosity is piqued about the unfolding events, the complete narrative of this incident will be disclosed in due course throughout the journey of this book. It is a stark reminder that disaster can strike unexpectedly in life, and it is your response to such situations that ultimately shape the outcome.

Understand the Power of Mindset

We have to develop habits so that the mysteries of the mind may not destroy us and gain profound insights into the power it wields over our actions and outcomes. We have to be stronger on the influence on the perceptions, decisions, and ultimately, the trajectory of personal and professional life. Prepare to expand your understanding of the profound impact mindset has on shaping your reality. Most of the situations or events are inevitable and can't be altered. The sudden death of a close relative may shake you, but you have to withstand the shock with the internal power of mind.

The Influence of Mindset on Personal Development

There is a symbiotic relationship between mindset and personal development. The way you perceive challenges and opportunities shapes your growth journey. Through real-life examples and compelling anecdotes, you can understand how cultivating a growth-oriented mindset can catalyse your personal development, empowering you to navigate the complexities of life with resilience and grace. A heavy loss in your business may invite sleepless nights or even inadequate relationship adjustment with your close relatives. You cannot survive if you do not adjust your mental agony due to the subject disaster.

Overcome Limiting Beliefs for Mindset Mastery

Confront the barriers that hinder your mindset mastery by addressing and dismantling limiting beliefs. Guide yourself through a process of self-discovery, helping you identify and challenge beliefs that may be holding you back. Armed with practical strategies, you will learn how to replace limiting beliefs with empowering ones, paving the way for a mindset that thrives on possibility and potential.

Overcoming limiting beliefs for mindset mastery involves recognizing and challenging negative thoughts or beliefs that hold you back. Here are some steps and examples to help you overcome limiting beliefs:

1. Identify Limiting Beliefs

    Example: "I'm not good enough to succeed in my career."

1. Question the Validity

    Ask yourself if there is evidence supporting or contradicting the belief.
    Example: "What specific evidence do I have that proves I'm not good enough? Can I recall instances where I have succeeded?"

3. Challenge Negative Self-Talk

    Replace negative thoughts with positive affirmations.
    Example: Replace "I can't do this" with "I can learn and improve with effort."

4. Visualize Success

Imagine yourself succeeding and visualize the positive outcomes.

Example: Picture yourself excelling in your career and enjoying the benefits of success.

5. Set Realistic Goals

Break down larger goals into smaller, achievable steps.

Example: Instead of aiming for a promotion immediately, set a goal to acquire new skills relevant to your career.

6. Seek Support

Talk to friends, mentors, or a coach who can provide encouragement and perspective.

Example: Share your doubts with a trusted friend or mentor, and listen to their supportive feedback.

7. Learn from Failure

View failures as opportunities for growth and learning.

Example: Instead of seeing a setback as proof of your inadequacy, analyse it objectively, extract lessons, and use it as a stepping stone for improvement.

8. Cultivate a Growth Mindset

Embrace challenges as opportunities to learn and grow.

Example: Instead of fearing challenges at work, see them as chances to develop new skills and expand your capabilities.

9. Affirmations and Positive Self-Talk

Repeat positive affirmations to reinforce a positive mindset.

Example: Affirmations like "I am capable and confident" can counteract beliefs of inadequacy.

10. Surround Yourself with Positivity

Engage with positive influences and environments.

Example: Attend events, read books, or connect with people who inspire and uplift you.

Practical Strategies for Unleashing the Power Within

Equip yourself with actionable strategies to unleash the full potential within. Use this as a toolkit of practical techniques, exercises, and mindset-shifting practices designed to empower you on your journey. From cultivating resilience to fostering a positive outlook, these strategies serve as the building blocks for mastering your mindset and conquering the challenges that lie ahead. Get ready to implement transformative changes and witness the ripple effect on every aspect of your life.

Action Points for Chapter

1. Embark on the Journey of Self-Discovery:

Recognize that this book serves as a gateway to profound self-discovery and empowerment.

Understand that transformative change begins within the mind, setting the stage for the exploration of mindset mastery.

2. Awaken and Harness Your Inner Potential:

Accept the affirmation that immense potential resides within you, waiting to be awakened and harnessed.

Internalize the concept that "Mindset Mastery" is a dynamic force shaping your perception of the world and the trajectory of your life.

3. Navigate the Corridors of Mindset Mastery:

Engage actively in the journey to uncover the keys to breaking free from self-imposed limitations.

Embrace the transformative exercises and strategies provided in the book to reshape your mindset and, consequently, your reality.

4. Understand the Power of Mindset through Real-Life Anecdotes:

Absorb the real-life narrative of the author's experience with unexpected challenges and the mental stress associated with it.

Reflect on the unfolding events to grasp the significance of mindset in shaping outcomes during challenging situations.

5. Learn Practical Strategies for Overcoming Limiting Beliefs:

Identify your limiting beliefs and question their validity.

Challenge negative self-talk through positive affirmations and visualization of success.

Set realistic goals, seek support, and view failures as opportunities for growth.

Cultivate a growth mindset and surround yourself with positivity.

Utilize the provided actionable strategies and exercises to unleash the power within and master your mindset.

CHAPTER TWO

Resilience Redefined: Thriving in Adversity

Within life's complex fabric, adversity is seamlessly an inevitable thread.

How we navigate through challenges and setbacks often determines our ability to not only survive but to thrive. With the concept of resilience, we can redefine it as more than just bouncing back from difficulties. It explores the profound capacity within individuals to not only withstand adversity but to harness it as a catalyst for personal growth and well-being.

In the 2008 Beijing Games, the accomplished swimmer Michael Phelps achieved a historic feat by becoming the first athlete to secure eight gold medals in a single Olympics within the realm of swimming. During his pursuit of the seventh gold medal, a significant obstacle emerged as he suffered a fractured hand. There was considerable apprehension that his quest for the eighth gold medal would be compromised, with his coach even cautioning against further participation in the competition. Undeterred, Phelps exhibited unwavering determination. Implementing targeted exercises to strengthen his legs, he not only persisted in the

competition but emerged victorious, securing his eighth gold medal in the event. His enduring legacy includes a memorable phrase that resonates to this day: he defined "WIN" as an acronym for "What's Important Now."

The Power Within - Exploring the Foundations of Resilience

Understanding resilience begins with a journey inward, exploring the innate strengths and capabilities that lie within individuals. It is the psychological and emotional foundations of resilience that work, shedding light on the power within each person to confront and overcome life's challenges. Through introspection and self-awareness, individuals can tap into their inner resilience, fostering a mindset that is essential for navigating the complexities of life.

Certain essential elements contribute to our ability to bounce back from adversity and thrive.

Let's explore some of these foundational aspects:

1. Resiliency Capacities

Social Competence:
This includes traits like responsiveness, cultural flexibility, empathy, effective communication, and a sense of humor.

Problem-Solving Skills:
Resilient individuals exhibit planning abilities, seek help when needed, and engage in critical and creative thinking.

Autonomy:
A strong sense of identity, self-efficacy, self-awareness, and the ability to distance oneself from negative influences.

Purpose and Optimism:
Having goals, educational aspirations, faith, and a belief in a bright future.

1. Environmental Protective Factors

Caring Relationships:

Compassionate, understanding, and respectful connections that establish safety and trust.

Belief in Growth and Development:

Recognizing the innate capacity for self-righting and transformation.

Opportunities for Participation and Power:

Environments that foster [1]resilience through relationships, beliefs, and inclusion.

Resilience operates at a deep structural level, influencing every interaction and intervention. It's about harnessing our inner strength and the supportive environments around us.

Navigating Life's Storms - Strategies for Building Emotional Resilience

Life's storms are inevitable, but how we weather them is a matter of emotional resilience. This section elucidates practical strategies for building and fortifying emotional resilience. From coping mechanisms to stress management techniques, it explores ways individuals can cultivate the mental fortitude needed to navigate the ups and downs of life. By mastering these strategies, individuals can develop a resilient mindset that enables them to confront adversity with grace and strength.

Let me give you some valuable insights on how to weather life's challenges with strength and grace.

Here are some practical strategies for cultivating emotional resilience.

1. Foster Optimism

Seek the silver linings hidden in life's challenges and maintain faith in your ability to overcome anything that comes your way.

2. Strengthen Social Connections

Surround yourself with positive people and role models who energize you. Quality relationships reinforce resilience[3].

3. Practice Self-Care

Prioritize your well-being by taking care of your physical, mental, and emotional health. Regular exercise, adequate rest, and mindfulness contribute to resilience[4].

4. Develop Problem-Solving Skills

Approach difficulties as opportunities for growth. Cultivate a solution-oriented mindset and learn from setbacks.

5. Cultivate Emotional Awareness

Understand and manage your emotions effectively. Emotional regulation skills help you maintain a positive mindset even during challenging times.

6. Seek Support

Build a support system of friends, family, or professionals who can provide encouragement and guidance.

7. Embrace Adaptability

Life is dynamic, and resilience involves adapting to change. Be flexible and open to new situations.

8. Practice Self-Compassion

Treat yourself with kindness and empathy. Acknowledge that setbacks are part of the journey and practice self-compassion.

Adaptability in Action - Embracing Change as a Catalyst for Growth

Change is a constant in life, and resilience is closely tied to one's ability to adapt. There is an importance of embracing change as a catalyst for personal growth. It explores how adaptability, flexibility, and a positive mindset can transform challenges into opportunities. Through real-life examples and case studies, you will gain insights into how adaptability in action can lead to transformative experiences, ultimately enhancing resilience.

Alexander Graham Bell, a Scottish-born Canadian-American inventor, scientist, and engineer was a renowned inventor of the telephone.

His mother's gradual deafness deeply affected him, beginning when he was only 12 years old. Despite this challenge, Bell pursued his passion for communication, ultimately revolutionizing the way people connect across distances.

Despite his limitations, Alexander Graham Bell's inventive spirit revolutionized communication, leaving an indelible mark on history.

Community Resilience - Strengthening Bonds in Times of Adversity

Resilience is not solely an individual endeavor; it thrives within the fabric of communities. This section delves into the concept of community resilience, highlighting the significance of building strong bonds and fostering a collective capacity to withstand adversity. Through shared experiences and mutual support, communities can create a resilient foundation that not only benefits individuals but also contributes to the overall strength and well-being of the community as a whole.

Mind-Body Harmony - The Role of Wellness in Resilience Building

A holistic approach to resilience recognizes the interconnectedness of mind and body. There is a vital role of wellness in building resilience, emphasizing the importance of a balanced and healthy lifestyle. From physical fitness to mindfulness practices, it delves into how nurturing mind-body harmony contributes to overall well-being and enhances the capacity to face life's challenges with resilience and strength.

Conclusion

We can seek to redefine resilience as a dynamic and multifaceted concept, encouraging everyone to explore the depths of inner strength, develop practical strategies for emotional resilience, embrace change as a catalyst for growth, strengthen community bonds, and prioritize mind-body harmony for a resilient and thriving life.

Action Points for Chapter

1. Explore Resilience Foundations:

    Undertake an inward journey to understand the psychological and emotional foundations of resilience.
    Recognize resilience capacities, including social competence, problem-solving skills, autonomy, and a sense of purpose and optimism.

2. Cultivate Essential Resilience Capacities:

    Develop social competence by honing traits like empathy, effective communication, and cultural flexibility.

Enhance problem-solving skills, autonomy, and a sense of purpose and optimism to fortify your resilience.

3. Leverage Environmental Protective Factors:

Foster caring relationships that establish safety and trust.
Embrace beliefs in growth and development, recognizing innate capacities for self-righting and transformation.
Seek environments that provide opportunities for participation and empowerment.

4. Build Emotional Resilience Strategies:

Foster optimism by seeking silver linings in challenges and maintaining faith in your ability to overcome.
Strengthen social connections with positive individuals and role models.
Prioritize self-care through physical, mental, and emotional well-being practices.
Develop problem-solving skills and a solution-oriented mindset.
Cultivate emotional awareness and effective emotion regulation.
Build a support system for encouragement and guidance.
Embrace adaptability, flexibility, and a positive mindset.

5. Embrace Change for Personal Growth:

Understand the importance of adaptability and flexibility in transforming challenges into opportunities.
Gain insights from real-life examples, such as Alexander Graham Bell's journey, showcasing adaptability as a catalyst for personal growth.

6. Strengthen Community Resilience:

Recognize resilience as a collective endeavor within communities.

Understand the significance of building strong bonds and fostering a collective capacity to withstand adversity.

Contribute to community well-being through shared experiences and mutual support.

7. Prioritize Mind-Body Harmony for Wellness:

Embrace a holistic approach to resilience by recognizing the interconnectedness of mind and body.

Understand the vital role of wellness in building resilience.

Implement practices such as physical fitness and mindfulness to nurture mind-body harmony.

8. Reflect and Implement:

Reflect on the concept of resilience as a dynamic and multifaceted concept.

Implement practical strategies for emotional resilience, embrace change for personal growth, strengthen community bonds, and prioritize mind-body harmony.

[1] Source: https://www.resiliency.com

CHAPTER THREE

Overcoming Overwhelm – Strategies for Mental Clarity

In the hustle and bustle of modern life, individuals often find themselves grappling with overwhelming emotions, stress, and the constant pressure to meet various demands. Therefore, it is very much necessary to think and design deeper idea ideas, practical insights, and actionable strategies to navigate through the complexities of life, fostering mental clarity and overall well-being. Let's explore the key elements to uncover effective approaches to overcome overwhelm and embrace a more balanced and resilient mindset.

Understanding the Roots: Identifying Sources of Overwhelm

In the pursuit of achieving mental clarity, it is crucial to get insight on a journey of self-discovery by understanding and identifying the roots of overwhelm. This is for familiarizing to help you recognize the various sources of stress and chaos in their lives, laying the foundation for effective strategies to overcome overwhelm.

Self-Reflection and Awareness

Encouraging self-reflection is the first step toward understanding the roots of overwhelm. You have to introspectively explore your thoughts, emotions, and daily experiences. By developing a heightened self-awareness, you can pinpoint specific triggers that contribute to feelings of overwhelm.

External Stressors

There are external factors that often contribute to overwhelm, such as work pressures, financial challenges, or relationship dynamics. By acknowledging and categorizing these external stressors, you can begin to devise targeted strategies for managing and mitigating your impact.

When your boss insulted you at your workplace and you had a sleepless night. Your partner in a business cheated you and you are constantly worrying about dealing with him or even boycotting. Your spouse did not agree over a trivial matter and it made you upset. This can be anything.

Internal Stressors

Internal stressors, such as negative self-talk, perfectionism, or unrealistic expectations, are dissected to help you understand how your thoughts and beliefs

contribute to overwhelm. Practical exercises and reflection prompts aid in uncovering and challenging these internal stressors. One of the negative comments on one of my books induced fear that my book may not be sold in the market. Later, my mentor explained that negative comments are also part of constructive critiques. I was convinced and the book became a best seller in due course.

Life Transitions and Changes

Life transitions, whether positive or negative, can be significant sources of overwhelm. I want to address how major life changes, such as career shifts, relocation, or personal milestones, can impact one's mental well-being. Strategies for adapting to change and managing associated stress are explored.

You settled down in the city with all your routines and all of a sudden you were transferred to another city as it was the requirement of your office, you may be upset and even think of leaving the job. You may sustain the change and you may get new opportunities and a better environment for your personal as well as career growth.

Unaddressed Emotions

Often, overwhelming feelings are rooted in unaddressed emotions. You may realize this when you recognize and express your emotions constructively. By fostering emotional intelligence, individuals can navigate challenges with greater resilience and clarity.

Time Management and Boundaries

Time-related stressors and challenges with setting boundaries can be explored. You can gain insights into effective time management techniques and strategies for establishing healthy boundaries in both personal and professional spheres, reducing the risk of feeling overwhelmed.

Social and Environmental Influences

The impact of social and environmental factors on mental well-being is deeply rooted. This includes examining how social relationships, societal expectations, and the physical environment contribute to overwhelm. Practical tips for cultivating a supportive social network and creating a conducive environment for mental clarity are crucial.

Pattern Recognition

Recognize the patterns of overwhelm. By identifying recurring themes and triggers, you can develop a proactive approach to managing stress. Your goal should be to empower yourself to anticipate and navigate overwhelming situations with greater ease and resilience.

Understanding the roots of overwhelm is a foundational step toward achieving mental clarity. By learning the various dimensions of stress and chaos, you can tailor your approach to overcoming overwhelm, creating a more resilient and balanced foundation for improved mental well-being.

Mindful Approaches: Cultivating Mental Clarity in Daily Life

Explore the transformative power of mindfulness as a tool for cultivating mental clarity in day-to-day living. This will offer practical techniques and exercises to integrate mindfulness into various aspects of life, fostering a heightened sense of awareness and presence. Learn to navigate challenges with a calm and focused mind, promoting mental resilience.

Focus on incorporating mindfulness practices into everyday routine to enhance mental clarity.

Let's break down the key components:

A. **Mindful Approaches: Adopting techniques and strategies that involve mindfulness. Mindfulness is the practice of being fully present and engaged in the current moment, without judgment. It often involves paying attention to your thoughts, feelings, and surroundings with heightened awareness.**

B. Cultivating Mental Clarity: Your goal should be to nurture and develop mental clarity. Mental clarity involves having a clear and focused mind, free from unnecessary distractions or clutter. It allows for better decision-making, increased self-awareness, and improved overall cognitive function.

C. In Daily Life: Emphasize the integration of mindfulness into everyday activities. Instead of being a separate practice reserved for specific times, the idea is to weave mindfulness into daily routines, such as during work, daily chores, or even leisure activities.

Organizational Mastery: Streamlining Tasks for Reduced Overwhelm

Efficiently manage tasks and responsibilities by mastering the art of organization. Adopt actionable strategies for streamlining daily activities, optimizing productivity, and reducing the burden of overwhelm. You can gain insights into creating effective systems that bring order to chaos, promoting a more structured and manageable lifestyle.

Consider yourself as a part of a software development company aiming for organizational mastery to streamline tasks and reduce overwhelm. The company might implement the following strategies:

a. **Project Management Tools:** Utilize advanced project management tools that allow teams to collaborate seamlessly, track progress, and manage tasks efficiently.

b. **Agile Methodology:** Adopt agile methodologies to break down complex projects into smaller, manageable tasks. This promotes flexibility, quick adaptation to changes, and continuous improvement.

c. **Training and Skill Development:** Invest in training programs to enhance the skills of employees. This can lead to a more capable workforce that can handle tasks more efficiently, reducing the likelihood of feeling overwhelmed.

d. Communication Protocols: Establish clear communication channels and protocols to ensure that information flows smoothly within the organization. This helps prevent misunderstandings and reduces the stress associated with miscommunication.

Stress Management Techniques: Building Resilience in Overwhelming Situations.

Equip yourself with a repertoire of stress management techniques designed to build resilience in the face of overwhelming situations. From relaxation exercises to cognitive-behavioral strategies, this may help you as a comprehensive toolkit for effectively managing stress. Learn to navigate challenges with grace, fostering mental strength and emotional well-being.

Creating Balance: Strategies for a Holistic Approach to Mental Well-being

Achieve a holistic approach to mental well-being by exploring strategies that promote balance in various facets of life. Find equilibrium between work, relationships, self-care, and leisure, fostering a sustainable and fulfilling lifestyle. Discover how to create a harmonious life that nurtures both mental and emotional well-being.

Action Points for Chapter

1. Self-Reflection and Awareness:

Engage in self-reflection to understand thoughts, emotions, and daily experiences.

Develop heightened self-awareness to pinpoint specific triggers causing overwhelm.

1. **Identify External Stressors:**

Acknowledge and categorize external stressors like work pressures and relationship dynamics.

Devise targeted strategies for managing and mitigating the impact of external stressors.

3. **Address Internal Stressors:**

Dissect internal stressors like negative self-talk, perfectionism, and unrealistic expectations.

Use practical exercises and reflection prompts to uncover and challenge these internal stressors.

4. **Navigate Life Transitions:**

Understand the impact of major life changes on mental well-being.

Develop strategies for adapting to change and managing associated stress.

5. **Cultivate Emotional Intelligence:**

Recognize and express emotions constructively.

Foster emotional intelligence to navigate challenges with resilience and clarity.

CHAPTER FOUR

Victorious Vulnerability – Embracing Imperfections

In a world that often glorifies perfection and celebrates flawlessness, there lies a profound beauty in acknowledging and embracing our vulnerabilities. We are, sometimes, challenged by the conventional notions of strength and success, encouraging us to see imperfections not as shortcomings, but as unique facets that contribute to the intricate mosaic of our identity.

There is a power of vulnerability as a catalyst for connection, resilience, and authenticity. Take it as a compass, guiding you through the terrain of self-acceptance and encouraging you to view your imperfections not as obstacles to overcome, but as stepping stones toward personal triumph.

Together, let us navigate the path of self-discovery, discovering the strength that emerges from vulnerability and the triumph that accompanies embracing imperfections. It is in acknowledging our flaws that we find the courage to truly shine, making our journey not just one of self-improvement but a celebration of the victorious beauty inherent in our very vulnerabilities.

The Power of Authenticity: Unveiling the Strength in Vulnerability

Get on a journey of self-discovery by understanding the transformative power of authenticity. Explores how embracing vulnerability allows individuals to unveil their true selves, fostering genuine connections and inner strength. Discover the profound impact of authenticity on mental and emotional well-being.

This is about the transformative potential of embracing the authentic self. Let us emphasize the true strength that lies in vulnerability, as it opens the door to genuine connections and personal growth. By shedding societal expectations and embracing authenticity, individuals unlock a reservoir of resilience and courage. Recognize vulnerability not as a weakness but as a source of power, leading to a more profound understanding of oneself and others. Authenticity is the key to unlocking the hidden strength within vulnerability, fostering resilience, and building meaningful connections.

Navigating Imperfection: A Journey Towards Personal Triumph

Explore the concept of imperfection as a stepping stone toward personal triumph. This may be difficult but endure to stay tuned to the process of navigating challenges, learning from mistakes, and embracing the

beauty found in imperfections. By reframing perspectives, individuals can turn setbacks into opportunities for growth and self-discovery.

Develop your insight on your path to self-discovery and growth by reframing imperfections as stepping stones toward triumph. Navigate the complex terrain of your flaws, learning to embrace them as integral parts of your identity rather than obstacles to success. Always emphasize a journey that may not be easy toward personal triumph. It is not about achieving perfection but about understanding, accepting, and leveraging imperfections.

Recognize the opportunity through navigating and embracing imperfections so that they can unlock your true potential. By reframing perceived weaknesses, individuals can discover hidden strengths, resilience, and authenticity. Grow a shift in mindset, from viewing imperfections as limitations to understanding them as essential components of a unique and fulfilling journey towards personal triumph. Understand deeply to promote self-compassion, and resilience, and learn that imperfections are not roadblocks but essential elements in the pursuit of personal growth and triumph.

Embracing Vulnerability: A Key to Resilience and Inner Strength

Embracing Vulnerability: A Key to Resilience and Inner Strength
Embracing vulnerability contributes to our emotional resilience and inner strength. Let's understand what it means and why it matters:

1. **Understanding Emotional Strength:**

i. Emotional strength isn't just about feeling good; it's about equipping ourselves with tools and techniques to navigate life's inevitable ups and downs with grace.
v. Think of emotional strength as your internal armour that protects you against stress, hardship, and emotional pain while allowing you to recover and grow from these experiences.

2. **Foundation of Resilience:**

v. **Building emotional strength starts with acknowledging your current feelings and understanding that it's okay to experience a wide range of emotions.**
v. **Self-acceptance serves as the foundation upon which resilience is built.**

3. **Mindfulness Meditation:**

v. As you develop your emotional muscles, mindfulness meditation can help you remain present and engaged with your experiences without being overwhelmed.

v. Remember that becoming emotionally stronger doesn't happen overnight, but with patience and practice, you can increase your resilience and enhance your mental health.

4. **Constructive Mindset:**

v. During tough times, maintaining a constructive mindset is crucial.

v. Simple practices like focusing on your breath or counting to ten can serve as your anchor, giving you a momentary pause to collect your thoughts and respond effectively to stress.

5. **Embracing Vulnerability:**

v. Initially uncomfortable, embracing vulnerability is a decisive step toward emotional growth.

v. By opening up about your feelings with trusted individuals, you reduce feelings of isolation and foster deeper connections.

v. Failure becomes a stepping stone for growth, and setbacks no longer derail your path to greater happiness.

Turning Weakness into Strength: The Triumph of Embracing Imperfections

Discover the transformative journey of turning perceived weaknesses into strengths. Let us understand and develop the skill through practical insights and strategies for reframing negative self-perceptions, empowering individuals to harness the triumph that comes from embracing imperfections.

Once upon a time, in a quiet neighbourhood, lived a young girl named Amelia[1]. Life seemed perfect for her—she was a star basketball player, had brilliant doctor parents, and academic achievements that shone brightly. But hidden within this colourful canvas was a brushstroke that made her stand out: a condition called hyponychia, where her fingers lacked nails. It was her "perfect flaw."

Amelia's parents reassured her that this uniqueness was cool, but the reactions from other kids painted a different picture. Whispers and stares created discomfort within her. She faced judgment and isolation, feeling like an alien. Her parents' encouragement clashed with the pain inflicted by peers who saw her as different.

Then, fate intervened. New neighbours moved in—Crystal and her mom, Mrs. Freeze. Crystal's warm demeanour contrasted sharply with her mother's icy attitude. A fateful encounter triggered a chain of events. Amelia discovered that Mrs. Freeze was now her basketball coach. Her belief in Amelia's potential sparked a transformation, replacing doubt with determination.

But life took an even more unexpected turn when Mrs. Freeze's true identity was revealed: she was Amelia's biological mother. As Amelia grappled with this revelation, she learned that imperfections could be bridges to strength. Her unique condition became a symbol of resilience, and her journey from rivalry to acceptance taught her the true meaning of family.

Amelia's story reminds us that embracing vulnerability and imperfections isn't weakness—it's a courageous choice that leads to resilience and inner fortitude. By opening up, we connect more deeply, love others, and allow ourselves to be loved fully.

Let us conclude that the courageous path will always lead to victorious vulnerability when you embrace authenticity. So, this leads to a more authentic and victorious way of living and navigating life with resilience, authenticity, and a sense of triumph.

Action Points for Chapter

1. **Cultivate Authenticity:**

Begin a journey of self-discovery by embracing the transformative power of authenticity.

Shed societal expectations to unlock resilience, courage, and genuine connections.

2. **Navigate Imperfections for Triumph:**

Reframe perspectives on imperfections, viewing them as stepping stones toward personal triumph.

Embrace the journey of navigating challenges, learning from mistakes, and finding beauty in imperfections.

3. **Embrace Vulnerability for Resilience:**

Understand emotional strength as the internal armor against life's challenges.

Build resilience on the foundation of self-acceptance and mindfulness meditation.

4. **Develop a Constructive Mindset:**

Cultivate a constructive mindset during tough times to effectively respond to stress.

Use simple practices like focusing on breath or counting to ten as anchors for emotional strength.

5. **Turn Weakness into Strength:**

Discover the transformative journey of turning perceived weaknesses into strengths.

Reframe negative self-perceptions through practical insights and strategies, harnessing triumph from embracing imperfections.

[1] https://www.psychologytoday.com

CHAPTER FIVE

Fearless Forward: Navigating Uncertainty

In the journey of life and progress, uncertainty is an unavoidable aspect, much like a constant companion whose presence shapes our experiences and decisions. It is a force that can either paralyze us with fear or serve as a powerful catalyst for growth and transformation. Let us discuss the significance of embracing the unknown, harnessing change, and thriving amidst challenges, illustrating how resilience, innovative thinking, and effective strategies can propel individuals forward in the face of uncertainty.

Consider a real-world example of a startup founder navigating the uncertain landscape of the business world. When launching a new venture, entrepreneurs often encounter unexpected challenges, market fluctuations, and unforeseen obstacles. Embracing the unknown, in this context, involves acknowledging that not every aspect of the business journey can be predicted or controlled. Rather than succumbing to fear or hesitation, successful entrepreneurs understand the need to adapt and pivot when necessary.

Harnessing change becomes crucial in such scenarios. For instance, a tech startup might realize that a shift in market trends requires a modification of its product or service offering. Instead of resisting this change, the company embraces it, tweaking its approach to align with evolving customer needs. This adaptability is not just a survival mechanism; it becomes a source of competitive advantage and innovation.

The power of resilience shines through in the face of setbacks and challenges. Imagine the same startup facing a financial downturn or a product launch that doesn't meet expectations. Resilience involves bouncing back from these setbacks, learning from failures, and maintaining the determination to continue the entrepreneurial journey. Successful individuals in various fields often attribute their achievements to the ability to persevere in the face of adversity.

Innovative thinking becomes a driving force for progress. Going back to our startup example, a company might innovate by exploring new technologies, redefining its business model, or creating unique partnerships to stay ahead in a competitive market. By fostering a culture of innovation, individuals, and organizations can turn uncertainty into an opportunity for growth and advancement.

Effective strategies act as a roadmap for navigating the uncertain terrain. Just as a seasoned explorer plans their

route and equip themselves with the necessary tools, individuals facing uncertainty need a strategic approach. This might involve thorough risk assessment, scenario planning, and a proactive mindset to anticipate challenges and capitalize on opportunities.

In essence, embracing the unknown, harnessing change, and thriving amidst challenges require a mindset that views uncertainty not as a hindrance but as a potential source of inspiration and growth. The combination of resilience, innovative thinking, and effective strategies empowers individuals to forge ahead, turning uncertainty into a pathway for personal and professional development.

Embracing Change: The Catalyst for Fearless Forward Movement

There is always a transformative nature of change and we can learn how embracing it can catalyze fearless progress. For discussing the psychological aspects of change, we can highlight its potential to open new doors, broaden perspectives, and create growth opportunities. Practical examples and case studies can give a deeper illustrative idea of how individuals and organizations can turn pivotal moments of change into stepping stones for success.

Consider the retail industry's transformation with the rise of e-commerce. Traditional brick-and-mortar retailers faced the challenge of adapting to online shopping trends. Companies like Walmart embraced this change by investing heavily in their e-commerce platforms, introducing click-and-collect services, and integrating technology to enhance the customer experience. This embrace of change allowed them not only to survive in the digital age but to thrive and compete with online giants.

Strategies for Success in the Face of Uncertainty

Understand the importance of a toolkit of strategies to navigate uncertainty effectively. It can provide knowledge about proactive planning, risk management, and the importance of adaptability. You will gain insights into decision-making processes that minimize risks and maximize potential gains. Real-world examples can be observed to showcase how strategic thinking can be applied to various situations, fostering a proactive and fearless approach to uncertainty.

Think that a company anticipates potential disruptions due to key personnel retiring or leaving the organization. There can be the following solution.

The HR department engages in strategic thinking by implementing succession planning. They identify high-potential employees, invest in training and development, and create a talent pipeline to fill critical roles. This proactive strategy ensures a smooth transition and minimizes the impact of personnel changes on organizational performance.

Cultivating a Resilient Mindset: The Key to Fearless Progress

Resilience is the linchpin for navigating uncertainty. It explores the psychological and emotional components of resilience, offering practical tips and exercises to cultivate a resilient mindset. You can learn how to bounce back from setbacks, maintain focus in the face of challenges, and build the mental fortitude needed to sustain forward momentum.

Picture the case of Mrs. Joan.

Joan, a mid-level manager in a dynamic tech company, faces unexpected professional setbacks. The company undergoes restructuring, leading to a downsizing of teams, and Joan finds herself facing the possibility of job loss. The uncertainty surrounding her career creates stress and anxiety.

Application of Cultivating a Resilient Mindset:

In this situation, Joan chooses to cultivate a resilient mindset, recognizing it as the key to fearless progress.

Embracing the Emotional Response:

Joan allows herself to acknowledge and process her emotions, understanding that it's natural to feel a sense of loss, disappointment, and uncertainty during a restructuring. By recognizing her emotions, she can better navigate and manage them.

Learning from Setbacks:

Instead of dwelling on the negative aspects, Joan reframes her perspective and sees the situation as an opportunity for personal and professional growth. She reflects on the skills and experiences she has gained in her current role, identifying areas for improvement and potential new directions for her career.

Building a Support Network:

Joan reaches out to colleagues, mentors, and friends for support. Cultivating a resilient mindset involves recognizing the value of a support network in overcoming challenges. She seeks advice, feedback, and encouragement, which helps her gain different perspectives and insights into potential opportunities.

Adapting to Change:

Understanding that change is inevitable, Joan adapts her mindset to embrace uncertainty as a constant in the professional world. She focuses on developing a flexible attitude, recognizing that adaptability is a valuable skill in an ever-changing work environment.

Setting Realistic Goals:

Joan sets short-term and long-term goals that align with her values and aspirations. By breaking down larger objectives into manageable steps, she creates a roadmap for progress. This not only provides a sense of direction but also allows her to celebrate small victories along the way.

Investing in Personal Development:

Cultivating a resilient mindset involves a commitment to continuous learning and personal development. Joan takes this opportunity to acquire new skills, attend relevant workshops, and explore areas of interest outside her current role. This proactive approach positions her for potential new opportunities within or outside the company.

Maintaining a Positive Outlook:

Despite the uncertainty, Joan consciously maintains a positive outlook. She focuses on her strengths, accomplishments, and the potential for growth in her career. A resilient mindset involves viewing setbacks as temporary hurdles rather than insurmountable obstacles.

Overcome Obstacles Amidst the Challenges of Tomorrow

This is a proactive and strategic approach for individuals and organizations for adopting to navigate and surmount challenges that are anticipated in the future. It involves preparing for uncertainties, building resilience, and developing effective strategies to tackle obstacles that may arise on the path to progress.

Let us break down the key elements as below.

1. **Anticipating Future Challenges:**

This aspect involves recognizing that the future is inherently uncertain and that challenges are likely to arise. It encourages individuals and organizations to engage in foresight, trend analysis, and scenario planning to identify potential obstacles they might face in the evolving landscape.

1. **Strategic Planning and Preparedness:**

Rather than reacting to challenges as they arise, the emphasis is on proactive strategic planning. This involves creating contingency plans, developing risk management strategies, and establishing protocols to address obstacles before they escalate. By being prepared, individuals and organizations can respond more effectively to unforeseen challenges.

3. **Building Resilience:**

Resilience plays a crucial role in overcoming obstacles. The topic involves exploring ways to build personal and organizational resilience, including cultivating a resilient mindset, fostering adaptability, and developing coping mechanisms. Resilience enables individuals and entities to bounce back from setbacks and persevere in the face of adversity.

4. **Creating Roadmaps for Obstacle Navigation:**

The topic suggests the importance of developing clear roadmaps or action plans to navigate specific obstacles. This might involve breaking down complex challenges into manageable steps, setting milestones, and establishing measurable goals. A well-defined roadmap provides a structured approach to overcoming obstacles.

5. **Learning from Past Experiences:**

Examining how individuals and organizations have successfully overcome challenges in the past is an integral part of the topic. Drawing lessons from historical examples or case studies helps in understanding effective strategies and learning from mistakes, contributing to a more informed and proactive approach to future obstacles.

6. **Innovative Problem-Solving:**

Overcoming obstacles often requires innovative thinking and creative problem-solving. This aspect of the topic explores how individuals can cultivate a mindset that embraces innovation, encouraging them to think outside the box and explore unconventional solutions to the challenges they may encounter.

7. **Collaboration and Support Networks:**

Acknowledging that tackling challenges is often a collective effort, the topic emphasizes the importance of collaboration and building strong support networks. Engaging with colleagues, mentors, and external partners can provide valuable insights, resources, and assistance in overcoming obstacles.

8. **Adapting to Change:**

Given that the challenges of tomorrow are likely to be dynamic and ever-evolving, adapting to change becomes a fundamental aspect of overcoming obstacles. The topic explores the importance of flexibility, openness to new ideas, and a willingness to adjust strategies in response to changing circumstances.

Action Points for Chapter

1. Embrace Change and Adaptability:

Acknowledge uncertainty as an integral part of life's journey.
Understand the transformative nature of change and its potential to catalyze fearless progress.

2. Learn from Real-world Examples:

Examine a real-world scenario of a startup founder navigating business uncertainties.
Recognize the importance of adaptability and pivoting in the face of unexpected challenges.

3. Cultivate Resilience in Setbacks:

Embrace resilience as a powerful tool in overcoming setbacks and challenges.

Learn from successful individuals who attribute their achievements to perseverance in the face of adversity.

4. Foster Innovative Thinking:

Understand innovative thinking as a driving force for progress in uncertain situations.

Explore examples of companies innovating to stay ahead in competitive markets.

5. Implement Effective Strategies:

Develop a strategic approach as a roadmap for navigating uncertainty.

Emphasize proactive planning, risk assessment, and a mindset to anticipate challenges and capitalize on opportunities.

CHAPTER SIX

Adaptive Agility – Transforming Challenges into Opportunities

In the ever-evolving landscape of today's dynamic world, businesses and leaders are continually faced with unprecedented challenges that demand a new level of adaptability and resilience. Adaptability is a crucial paradigm shift that empowers individuals and organizations to not only navigate change but also transform challenges into opportunities.

I want to share a significant experience that involved a major incident of engine failure due to a thread getting sucked into the air intake, resulting in a complete engine failure of the helicopter. The aircraft had to be grounded, and the damaged engine was sent to Hindustan Aeronautical Limited for overhaul.

After a series of inquiries, I was declared innocent regarding the incident as there was no malicious intent or possibility of sabotage. However, I experienced significant stress, realizing that I indirectly bore responsibility for the sustained damage, causing a loss of $160,000 to the organization. Another aircraft required servicing, as we anticipated an inspection by the Air

Marshal of the commands. Despite the stress and strain, I worked continuously for 72 hours without a break, catching only a couple of hours of sleep in the bay and even skipping meals.

The aircraft was successfully prepared for VIP moments, and later, the visiting dignitary inquired about the readiness of another aircraft, which had been arranged for his sorties. One of the supervisors informed him that I was responsible for the complete service of the helicopter used for his flights. Subsequently, I received appreciation from the Air Officer Commanding and was relieved of all charges of making mistakes. This acknowledgment gave me a significant boost and alleviated all the stress I had been under.

I challenged myself against time and completed the task of preparing the aircraft in record time. I was able to transform challenges into opportunities, and to this day, I take pride in my dedicated efforts during that challenging period.

Let us discuss some essential elements of understanding, harnessing, and thriving amidst uncertainty, fostering a culture of innovation and flexibility.

Understanding Adaptive Agility: Navigating Change in a Dynamic Environment

Adaptive Agility gocs beyond mere flexibility; it is the art of embracing change as a constant in the dynamic environment of today's world. I want to explore the core principles that define Adaptive Agility, understanding how to anticipate, respond, and even lead in times of flux. Navigating change becomes an opportunity rather than a hurdle, as we uncover the tools and mindset necessary to thrive in the face of uncertainty.

Let me share a real-life time story of an Indian Cricketer.

At a turning point in his life, Yuvraj Singh, the renowned cricketer, faced a formidable opponent off the cricket pitch — cancer. The diagnosis led him to the Cancer Research Institute, where he embarked on a challenging journey of treatment.

Enduring chemotherapy sessions and specific medications, Yuvraj confronted the formidable malignant tumor that had invaded his body. Yet, with the expertise of medical professionals and a resilient spirit, the doctors classified the tumor as malignant but curable.

In the broader context of overcoming adversity and inspiring resilience, Yuvraj Singh's legacy shines bright. His commitment to fitness and unwavering resilience serves as a profound inspiration, transcending the boundaries of the cricket pitch. Yuvraj's journey not only underscores the triumph over a life-threatening ailment but also serves as a testament to the human spirit's indomitable will to conquer challenges, both within and outside the sporting arena.

The Power of Resilience: Transforming Challenges into Growth Opportunities

Resilience is the cornerstone of Adaptive Agility. This section delves into the transformative power of resilience, demonstrating how challenges can serve as fertile ground for personal and organizational growth. By understanding the mechanisms of resilience, individuals and businesses can not only endure challenges but harness them as catalysts for innovation, learning, and lasting success.

Suman Singh (India) embarked on her acting journey with the television series "Manmohini" in the year 2020. Although her initial foray into the entertainment industry included roles as a background artist in television serials and films, it was her unwavering determination that propelled her to explore the expansive potential of online streaming platforms.

However, amidst her professional pursuits, Suman encountered a formidable challenge – a battle with cancer. Undeterred by this adversity, she emerged as a resilient figure and a beacon of hope, standing as a breast cancer survivor. Suman's triumph over the intricate path of cancer has positioned her as a passionate advocate for early detection and prevention.

Having navigated the complexities of her cancer journey, Suman underscores the paramount importance of regular medical check-ups and health screenings. Her fervent advocacy revolves around the critical concept of catching cancer in its nascent stages, emphasizing that early intervention significantly enhances the likelihood of a positive outcome.

In the face of personal trials, Suman Singh not only demonstrates resilience but also dedicates herself to raising awareness about the importance of timely screenings and proactive health measures. Her journey serves as an inspiring testament to the transformative power of determination and the significance of promoting early intervention in the fight against cancer.

Strategies for Adaptive Leadership: Thriving Amidst Uncertainty

Indian cricketer Kapil Dev serves as a compelling example of adaptive leadership in a dynamic environment. Kapil Dev's captaincy during the 1983 Cricket World Cup is a notable instance of his leadership prowess.

In a dynamic and uncertain sporting environment, Kapil Dev exhibited unique leadership skills. During the World Cup, India faced challenges, and their chances were considered slim. However, Kapil Dev adopted an adaptive leadership approach. Instead of succumbing to the pressure, he inspired and guided his team with a proactive and flexible mindset.

One significant moment was India's match against Zimbabwe, where the team faced a precarious situation. Kapil Dev, demonstrating adaptability, not only motivated his players but also made crucial strategic decisions, turning the challenge into an opportunity. His proactive approach and flexibility helped the team overcome uncertainties and eventually win the World Cup against the odds.

Kapil Dev's leadership style fostered a culture of continual improvement and excellence within the team. His ability to adapt to changing circumstances, inspire his players, and strategically navigate challenges showcases the essence of adaptive leadership. By embracing this approach, Kapil Dev not only led India to a historic victory but also left a lasting legacy as a leader who thrived in dynamic and uncertain environments.

Turning Disruptions into Advantages: A Guide to Adaptive Problem-solving

Disruptions are inevitable, but they can also be sources of innovation and advantage. In this concluding part, I would like to advise that adaptive problem-solving skills can be learned and applied in real-life situations by reframing disruptions as opportunities. individuals and organizations can develop effective strategies to not only overcome challenges but leverage them for strategic advantage, ensuring a sustained and prosperous future.

There is a Chinese proverb that goes like this,

"The gem cannot be polished without friction, nor man perfected without trials."

It encapsulates the profound concept that both precious gems and individuals undergo challenges and hardships to achieve their full potential.

The Gem Cannot Be Polished Without Friction

It draws a metaphor between a gemstone and personal development. To enhance the beauty and shine of a gem, it needs to undergo a process of polishing. This involves friction, a deliberate and controlled abrasion that smooth out imperfections, reveals the true brilliance of the gem, and ultimately transforms it into a valuable, polished entity. In the context of personal growth, challenges and difficulties can be seen as the necessary "friction" those shapes and refines an individual.

Nor Man Perfected Without Trials

It also directly applies the metaphor to human experiences. Just as a gem undergoes polishing, individuals go through trials and tribulations in their lives. Trials, challenges, and difficulties are seen as essential elements in the process of perfecting or refining a person. These experiences test one's resilience, strength, and character, leading to personal growth, maturity, and a more refined version of oneself.

Overall Meaning

Facing and overcoming challenges is an integral part of personal development and growth. Similar to how a gem needs friction to become polished, individuals need trials and difficulties to reach their full potential. It conveys the idea that adversities, rather than being obstacles, are opportunities for refinement and perfection, shaping individuals into resilient, stronger, and more capable beings.

Encourage yourself to embrace challenges and difficulties as opportunities for growth rather than setbacks with the transformative power of adversity and facing and overcoming trials. The resilience and strength that can be cultivated through confronting life's challenges and, ultimately, emerging as a more polished and perfected individual.

Action Points for Chapter

1. **Embrace Adaptive Agility:**

Understand adaptive agility as more than flexibility; it's about embracing change as a constant.

Explore core principles that define adaptive agility, emphasizing anticipation, response, and leadership in dynamic environments.

1. **Learn from Real-life Stories:**

   Draw inspiration from real-life stories like the Indian Cricketer Yuvraj Singh and actor Suman Singh.

   Understand how individuals facing adversity can transform challenges into opportunities through resilience and determination.

3. **Harness the Power of Resilience:**

   Recognize resilience as the cornerstone of adaptive agility.

   Explore how resilience can catalyze personal and organizational growth by turning challenges into catalysts for innovation and success.

4. **Study Adaptive Leadership:**

   Examine the adaptive leadership of Indian cricketer Kapil Dev during the 1983 Cricket World Cup.

   Identify leadership skills, proactive mindset, and flexibility as essential components of adaptive leadership in uncertain environments.

5. **Develop Adaptive Problem-solving Skills:**

   Acknowledge disruptions as inevitable but transformable into sources of innovation.

   Learn adaptive problem-solving skills to reframe disruptions as opportunities, ensuring a sustained and prosperous future.

Inner Strength Blueprint: Building a Solid Mental Foundation

We are in the crucial task of building a solid mental foundation. Let us explore the various components that contribute to inner strength, providing you with insights and practical strategies to fortify mental resilience.

The central idea for building inner strength revolves around the concept of building strong foundations before seeking growth and success.

I want to emphasize the importance of going deeper before aiming higher in any area of your work or field. I want to urge individuals to invest in their health, finances, friendships, and network reserves proactively, rather than waiting for challenges to force them to become strong.

There is a significance of clear self-identity, ethical achievement, and building a life based on strong foundations, emphasizing that success should not just be about results but also about the journey and the values one upholds. I want to encourage a mindset of continuous learning, preparation, and fortification for future challenges, creating a resilient and steadfast life.

Let us see some of the detailed ideas for building a strong mental foundation.

Understanding the Foundations: Exploring the Components of Inner Strength

To cultivate a robust foundation of inner strength, consider the following key components.

Self-awareness: Begin by delving into a deep understanding of yourself – your values, beliefs, and motivations. This introspection lays the groundwork for building resilience and navigating challenges with authenticity.

Emotional intelligence: Strengthen your ability to recognize and manage your emotions effectively. Developing emotional intelligence enhances interpersonal relationships, fosters empathy, and enables you to respond thoughtfully to both successes and setbacks.

Mindfulness and Presence: Incorporate mindfulness practices into your daily routine. Cultivating a present-moment awareness helps reduce stress, enhances focus, and fosters a greater sense of inner peace.

Adaptability: Embrace change as a constant in life. Developing adaptability allows you to navigate uncertainties with grace, turning challenges into opportunities for growth.

Positive Mindset: Foster a positive outlook on life. Cultivate optimism and gratitude, focusing on the silver linings even in difficult situations. A positive mindset contributes significantly to inner strength.

Resilience: Acknowledge setbacks as part of the journey and develop the resilience to bounce back from adversity. Embracing challenges as learning experiences fortifies your inner strength over time.

Connection with Others: Build a supportive network of relationships. Strong connections with friends, family, and community provide emotional support and contribute to a sense of belonging.

Continuous Learning: Adopt a mindset of continuous growth and learning. Seeking new knowledge and experiences contributes to personal development, broadening your perspective and enhancing your inner strength.

Values Alignment: Ensure that your actions align with your core values. Living by your principles creates a sense of purpose and integrity, forming a sturdy foundation for inner strength.

Physical Well-being: Prioritize your physical health through regular exercise, balanced nutrition, and sufficient rest. Physical well-being contributes significantly to mental resilience and overall inner strength.

Cultivating Resilience: Strategies for Building Mental Toughness

Cultivating resilience involves the intentional development of mental toughness, enabling individuals to navigate challenges with strength and adaptability. Resilience is not an innate trait but rather a set of skills and strategies that can be cultivated over time.

One key aspect of building mental toughness is developing a growth mindset. Embracing challenges as opportunities for learning and growth, individuals with a growth mindset view setbacks as temporary and use them to fuel personal development. This shift in perspective enhances resilience by fostering a proactive approach to difficulties.

Effective coping mechanisms are integral to resilience. Developing healthy coping strategies, such as mindfulness, deep breathing, or positive self-talk, helps manage stress and adversity. Mindfulness, in particular, encourages individuals to stay present in the moment, reducing anxiety about the future and regret about the past.

Social support plays a crucial role in building mental toughness. Cultivating strong connections with friends, family, or a community provides a support system during challenging times.

Sharing experiences and seeking advice from others fosters a sense of belonging and reinforces emotional well-being.

Adaptability is another cornerstone of resilience. Embracing change and developing flexibility in response to unexpected circumstances contribute to mental toughness. This adaptability allows individuals to navigate uncertainties with a constructive mindset, turning challenges into opportunities for growth.

Setting realistic goals and breaking them down into manageable steps is essential for building mental toughness. Achieving smaller milestones provides a sense of accomplishment, reinforcing confidence and perseverance in the face of larger challenges.

Furthermore, self-care practices contribute significantly to resilience. Prioritizing physical well-being through regular exercise, sufficient sleep, and a balanced diet fosters mental and emotional stability. Taking time for activities that bring joy and relaxation also contributes to overall resilience.

Cultivating resilience involves a holistic approach that integrates a growth mindset, effective coping mechanisms, social support, adaptability, goal-setting, and self-care. By actively engaging in these strategies, individuals can build mental toughness, empowering themselves to navigate life's inevitable challenges with resilience and strength.

Mindset Matters: Shaping a Positive and Empowering Mental Attitude

There is a profound impact that our mental attitude and perspective can have on our overall well-being and success. Shaping a positive and empowering mental attitude is a transformative process that influences how we approach challenges, setbacks, and everyday life.

At its core, mindset refers to the set of beliefs, perceptions, and attitudes that shape our thinking patterns and behaviors. A positive mindset is characterized by optimism, resilience, and a belief in one's ability to learn and grow. It involves viewing challenges as opportunities for growth rather than insurmountable obstacles.

The power of a positive mindset lies in its ability to shape outcomes. Individuals with a positive mental attitude are more likely to approach tasks with enthusiasm and determination, leading to increased motivation and productivity. This mindset fosters a solution-oriented approach, where setbacks are seen as temporary and opportunities to learn and improve.

Moreover, a positive mindset contributes to emotional well-being. It helps individuals manage stress, overcome adversity, and maintain a sense of balance and perspective in the face of life's uncertainties. The impact extends beyond personal well-being; it influences how individuals interact with others, fostering positive relationships and a supportive social environment.

Shaping an empowering mental attitude involves self-awareness and intentional efforts to challenge and reframe negative thoughts. Techniques such as mindfulness, gratitude practices, and affirmations play a crucial role in cultivating a positive mindset. Mindfulness encourages living in the present moment, reducing anxiety about the future, or dwelling on past challenges. Gratitude practices shift focus towards appreciating the positive aspects of life, fostering a sense of contentment.

"Mindset Matters" is a reminder that our thoughts are not passive; they actively shape our experiences. By consciously choosing a positive and empowering mental attitude, individuals can enhance their overall quality of life, build resilience in the face of adversity, and create a foundation for continuous personal growth and success. In essence, mindset becomes a powerful tool for navigating life's journey with optimism, purpose, and a belief in one's capacity to thrive.

Emotional Agility: Navigating Challenges with Grace and Self-Awareness

The subject agility encapsulates the concept of adeptly managing one's emotions in the face of life's challenges. This skill involves the capacity to recognize, understand, and adapt to emotions, allowing individuals to respond with flexibility and resilience. Emotional agility goes beyond the conventional notion of emotional intelligence, emphasizing not just understanding emotions but also navigating them with finesse.

In the realm of emotional agility, self-awareness plays a pivotal role. Individuals with emotional agility possess a keen understanding of their emotional landscape, acknowledging both positive and negative feelings without judgment. This self-awareness lays the foundation for effective emotional regulation and empowers individuals to make choices aligned with their values rather than succumbing to impulsive reactions.

Grace in the context of emotional agility suggests a composed and elegant approach to handling emotions. Instead of being overwhelmed by challenges, emotionally agile individuals gracefully pivot and adapt, viewing setbacks as opportunities for growth. This concept encourages individuals to embrace discomfort, allowing them to learn from difficult emotions and experiences.

In essence, emotional agility is a dynamic and adaptive approach to emotions, promoting a nuanced understanding of oneself and others. It equips individuals with the skills to navigate the complexities of life with resilience, poise, and a profound sense of self-awareness, fostering personal growth and well-being.

Tools for Inner Harmony: Practices to Strengthen Your Mental Foundation

In the pursuit of mental well-being, incorporating tools for inner harmony becomes paramount. These practices serve as anchors, reinforcing the core of our mental foundation. Mindfulness meditation, a powerful tool, encourages living in the present moment, fostering self-awareness and reducing stress. This practice enables individuals to navigate the complexities of daily life with a sense of clarity and tranquility.

Journaling emerges as a reflective practice, allowing one to express thoughts and emotions, fostering a deeper understanding of the self. Through written introspection, individuals can identify patterns, set goals, and track personal growth over time. Breathwork techniques, such as deep breathing and controlled breath patterns, serve as immediate stress relievers, promoting emotional regulation and mental resilience.

Cultivating a positive mindset stands as a fundamental tool for inner harmony. Gratitude practices, affirmations, and focusing on silver linings in challenging situations contribute to a more optimistic outlook. The incorporation of cognitive behavioral techniques aids in challenging negative thought patterns, promoting a healthier mental state.

Connection with others becomes a powerful tool, emphasizing the importance of supportive relationships. Engaging in open communication, active listening, and nurturing social bonds strengthens the mental foundation by providing emotional support and fostering a sense of belonging.

Let me conclude, these tools for inner harmony collectively create a toolkit for mental resilience, offering individuals the means to build a robust foundation, navigate life's challenges, and cultivate enduring mental well-being.

Action Points for Chapter

1. **Deep Self-Exploration:**

Invest time in understanding your values, beliefs, and motivations.

Foster self-awareness as the groundwork for building inner strength and resilience.

1. **Emotional Intelligence Enhancement:**

Develop skills to recognize and manage emotions effectively.

Prioritize emotional intelligence for improved interpersonal relationships and thoughtful responses to challenges.

3. **Mindfulness Integration:**

Incorporate mindfulness practices into daily routines.

Cultivate present-moment awareness to reduce stress, enhance focus, and foster inner peace.

4. **Adaptability Cultivation:**

Embrace change as a constant and develop adaptability.

View uncertainties as opportunities for personal growth and resilience.

5. **Positive Mindset Development:**

Foster a positive outlook on life.

Cultivate optimism, gratitude, and a focus on silver linings, contributing significantly to inner strength.

CHAPTER EIGHT

Limitless Learning: Growing Through Life's Lessons

In the grand tapestry of life, each experience, challenge, and triumph we encounter serves as a potential lesson waiting to be learned. There is a profound concept of limitless learning, emphasizing the transformative power that continuous learning which can have on our personal and professional growth. Let us learn some intricacies of perpetual learning, the significance of embracing a growth mindset, and the invaluable lessons that accompany us throughout our lifelong journey.

In the ever-evolving landscape of our existence, we find ourselves navigating a world of rapid change, where progress unfolds at an astonishing pace. From the clunky rotary phones of yesteryears to the sleek smartphones that now reside in our pockets, the journey has been nothing short of remarkable. Yet, amidst this whirlwind of transformation, there lies a profound truth: learning is the key to thriving.

The Acceleration of Progress

Consider the shift from 2015 to 2020—a mere five years—and observe the seismic changes. We've witnessed technological leaps, cultural shifts, and an explosion of information. The gap between then and now dwarfs the difference between 1995 and 2000. Our lives are both enriched and challenged by this relentless progress.

The Art of Learning

In this era of boundless information, the ability to learn swiftly and effectively is paramount. When knowledge becomes virtually infinite, those who master the art of learning gain a significant advantage. It's not just about absorbing facts; it's about processing them in impactful ways. Imagine a mental superpower—an ability to discover, comprehend, and synthesize information at lightning speed.

The Divide

Society today reflects a growing divide: those who learn well and those who struggle. This chasm manifests not only in income disparities but also in health, well-being, relationships, and addiction rates. The crux lies in helping people learn how to learn—to enhance our capacity to synthesize new knowledge.

Becoming a Lifelong Learner

Here are some strategies to embrace lifelong learning:

Become an Information Omnivore

Break free from habitual sources. Seek diverse perspectives. Read news from different viewpoints. Challenge your assumptions.

Screen Out Noise

Not all information is valuable. Sharpen your discernment. Filter out the irrelevant and focus on what truly matters.

Challenge Assumptions

Growth occurs when we question our beliefs. Be open to unlearning and relearning.

Life's Lessons: Our Greatest Teachers

Life, too, is a relentless teacher. Its lessons arrive uninvited, often disguised as hardships. Yet, within these trials lie resilience, patience, and perseverance. We learn to adapt, to rise after every fall, and to evolve into our best selves.

The Power of Perpetual Learning

In our swiftly changing world, where the Fourth Industrial Revolution unfolds before our eyes, the concept of perpetual learning emerges as a beacon of opportunity. Let us drive deep into this transformative paradigm—one that transcends traditional education and embraces continuous growth.

A. **The Accelerated Pace of Disruption**

The pace of disruption has reached unprecedented levels. Technology evolves, business models shift, and career paths blur. In this dynamic landscape, the need for perpetual learning is no longer a luxury; it is the new normal. We stand at the intersection of knowledge and adaptability, where our ability to learn becomes our greatest asset.

A. **Orchestrating Talent Ecosystems**

Universities, community colleges, vocational institutions, online course providers, and entrepreneurial challenges—all converge in a talent ecosystem. In this model, universities play the role of orchestrators. They collaborate with employers and industry, ensuring a steady supply of skilled talent. The boundaries between education and employment blur, creating a fluid exchange of knowledge and expertise.

C. Fueling Continuous Employability

Perpetual learning fuels continuous employability. It's not merely about acquiring skills; it's about applying them. Deliberate practice, self-assessment, and improvement become our compass. Experts remain perpetual learners, adapting mental models to solve new challenges. When we stop learning, we cease to be experts.

D. Business Impact

In the corporate realm, perpetual learning directly impacts productivity and job satisfaction. Employees who leverage their strengths are more productive and exhibit lower rates of absenteeism and turnover. It's a win-win—a virtuous cycle where learning enhances performance.

E. A Collaborative Future

Imagine a future where educational institutions, employers, and individuals collaborate seamlessly. They create synergistic consumption models, ensuring that skills remain renewable. This commitment to lifelong learning transcends age, benefiting youth, displaced workers, and the underemployed.

Perpetual learning is not a solitary pursuit; it's a collective endeavor. As we navigate the uncharted waters of progress, let us embrace perpetual learning—the catalyst for our limitless potential.

Embracing a Growth Mindset in Life's Classroom

Life's journey is an ever-evolving classroom, presenting us with challenges, opportunities, and lessons that shape our personal and professional growth. Adopting a growth mindset is akin to donning the lens of continuous learning, resilience, and adaptability.

A growth mindset is a belief that one's abilities and intelligence can be developed through dedication, effort, and learning. This perspective contrasts with a fixed mindset, which sees abilities as inherent and unchangeable. In life's classroom, those with a growth mindset thrive on challenges, seeing them as opportunities to learn and improve. They embrace setbacks as stepping stones to success and view criticism as constructive feedback to enhance their skills.

One of the key aspects of cultivating a growth mindset is the understanding that failures are not final, but rather temporary setbacks on the path to mastery. This mindset fosters perseverance and a willingness to confront difficulties, as individuals recognize that their abilities can be developed through dedication and hard work.

Moreover, a growth mindset encourages a love for learning. In life's dynamic classroom, new information, technologies, and experiences are constantly emerging. Embracing a growth mindset means actively seeking out opportunities to expand one's knowledge, even if it means stepping outside one's comfort zone.

In relationships, a growth mindset can transform conflicts into learning experiences. Instead of viewing disagreements as insurmountable obstacles, individuals with a growth mindset see them as chances to understand different perspectives and improve communication skills.

In essence, embracing a growth mindset in life's classroom is a transformative approach to facing the inevitable challenges and uncertainties that come our way. It empowers individuals to continually develop their abilities, adapt to change, and navigate the ever-evolving landscape of personal and professional growth. As we embrace this mindset, we not only enrich our own lives but contribute positively to the collective wisdom of the broader classroom we all share.

Lessons are Lifelong Allies

Life unfolds as a continuous series of experiences, each presenting valuable lessons that, when embraced, become lifelong allies on our journey. These lessons come in various forms — successes, failures, joys, and challenges — all contributing to the rich tapestry of our existence.

Lessons serve as guides, illuminating the path forward with the wisdom gained from past encounters. Successes celebrate our strengths and capabilities, affirming the choices and efforts that lead to positive outcomes. Failures, on the other hand, are potent teachers, offering insights into areas that require growth and improvement. Together, these experiences form a dynamic curriculum that shapes our character, resilience, and understanding of the world.

Embracing the idea that lessons are lifelong allies requires a mindset open to learning from every circumstance. Whether navigating personal relationships, professional endeavors, or facing unexpected twists of fate, recognizing the inherent teachings in each situation is crucial. Life's lessons equip us with the tools needed to navigate future challenges and make informed decisions, fostering personal development and growth.

Moreover, lessons connect us to a broader human experience, as shared wisdom is passed down through generations. Learning from the experiences of others becomes a source of inspiration and guidance, providing a collective reservoir of knowledge to draw upon in times of need.

In essence, lessons are not just fleeting occurrences; they are enduring companions on our life's journey. By cherishing and internalizing these teachings, we transform them into invaluable allies, shaping a narrative of continual self-discovery and improvement. As we navigate the complexities of existence, let us remain open to the profound wisdom that lessons offer, for in them, we find the keys to unlocking the full potential of our lives.

Navigating Challenges: A Pathway to Continuous Growth

Life's journey is marked by a series of challenges that, when faced with resilience and determination, become stepping stones toward continuous personal and professional growth. Challenges are not roadblocks but rather invitations to discover our inner strength, develop problem-solving skills, and adapt to the ever-changing landscape of life.

In the face of adversity, individuals often unearth hidden reserves of resilience and creativity. Challenges force us to think critically, explore new perspectives, and devise innovative solutions. Each obstacle encountered is an opportunity to learn, adapt, and emerge stronger on the other side. The process of overcoming challenges cultivates a mindset of perseverance, teaching us that setbacks are not defeats but rather integral parts of the journey toward success.

Moreover, navigating challenges fosters self-discovery. It is in moments of difficulty that we often uncover untapped potential, resilience, and capacities we didn't know we possessed. Challenges serve as mirrors reflecting our character, values, and priorities, guiding us to align our actions with our aspirations.

Continuous growth is not only about reaching new heights but also about the transformative journey undertaken in the face of challenges. Embracing difficulties as catalysts for improvement propels us forward, ensuring that we evolve into more resilient, adaptable, and resourceful individuals.

In essence, navigating challenges is not merely an unavoidable aspect of life; it is a deliberate and essential part of the human experience. As we confront and conquer challenges, we pave the way for continuous growth, evolving into the best versions of ourselves. The journey is not always smooth, but it is in the twists and turns, ups and downs, that we find the true essence of our potential and the limitless possibilities for growth that lie ahead.

Wisdom in Every Experience: The Journey of Limitless Learning

Wisdom is the culmination of lessons learned, experiences embraced, and challenges overcome. Lastly let us summarize the essence of the limitless learning journey, emphasizing the wisdom gained through a life dedicated to continuous growth. By recognizing the interconnectedness of experiences and lessons, we unveil the true depth of our potential and embark on a journey of lifelong wisdom acquisition.

Together, let us break the mental barriers that limit our learning potential and unlock the doors to a life of limitless growth and success.

Action Points for Chapter

1. **Embrace Lifelong Learning:**

   Cultivate a mindset of perpetual learning in both personal and professional aspects of life.

   Actively seek out diverse sources of information and challenge assumptions to broaden perspectives.

2. **Filter Information Effectively:**

   Develop the ability to discern valuable information from noise.

   Regularly assess and refine your information sources to stay focused on what truly matters.

3. **Challenge Assumptions:**

Foster a growth mindset by questioning and challenging your beliefs.

Be open to unlearning and relearning, viewing setbacks as opportunities for improvement.

4. Fuel Continuous Employability:

Understand that perpetual learning is essential for continuous employability.

Practice deliberate skill application, self-assessment, and improvement to stay relevant in a dynamic job market.

5. Cultivate a Collaborative Future:

Envision and actively contribute to a collaborative future where education, employment, and individuals seamlessly interact.

Recognize the collective nature of perpetual learning, benefiting individuals of all ages and diverse backgrounds.

CHAPTER NINE

Resonance of Redemption: A Tale of Triumph over Mental Abyss

At the outset of this book, you were introduced to the captivating narratives of my friends and relatives. Allow me to contribute one more intriguing and final story.

In the autumn of 1975, the small village of Latipur in the heart of Gujarat (India) was ablaze with fervor. The air was thick with anticipation as Navaratri approached, and the Latipur Boricha Raas Mandal (a dedicated team of folk dance) prepared for a grand performance at Boricha Vaas(the village street). The villagers gathered under the canopy of the starry night, their faces radiant with excitement, but the weight of this impending celebration bore down heavily on one individual: Karan.

Karan, a soul woven into the tapestry of village Latipur, was entrusted with a singular, pivotal task – to sing for the performance. As the day of the event neared, anxiety gripped his heart, and he couldn't help but feel overwhelmed by the gravity of the moment. The raucous rhythm of drumsticks seemed to thunder in his mind, echoing his mounting dread.

And then, as fate would have it, the announcement came like a thunderclap. A hush fell upon the crowd, and all eyes turned toward the organizer, who delivered the news that Karan, the voice of this grand celebration, had been struck down by an acute headache, rendering him incapable of singing. Karan lay immobilized, tears of anguish welling in his eyes. His body lay motionless, a mere spectator to the world around him, while his heart and soul cried out in silence.

Amid this profound despair, Karan found himself entangled in the treacherous labyrinth of his thoughts. It was a darkness he could not escape. It wasn't until, decades later, when he delved into the intricacies of the human mind during his pursuit of a master's degree in psychology, that he understood the crippling grip of the depression he had experienced that fateful night.

The threads of his thoughts had woven a suffocating cocoon around his spirit, stifling him, and robbing him of the breath of life. Even as his elder brother, compassionate teacher, loyal friends, and wise elders of the village surrounded him with love and care for a week, the shadows of his despair refused to dissipate. Karan remained locked in the prison of his mind.

But in the depths of despair, a glimmer of hope emerged. A relative, with a heart full of concern and a dash of faith, took Karan to the sacred abode of Maternal

Goddess Gatral at Jam Dudhai one of the villages of Gujarat. There, in the presence of divine energy, Karan's maternal uncle took it upon himself to meditate and invoke the mystical forces.

Chanting ancient mantras, he performed a mesmerizing ritual, swirling a copper pot filled with sacred water above Karan's body before finally drinking from it. The mystical dance of devotion and faith was performed, and something inexplicable transpired. As the minutes ticked away,

Karan was awakened with normal senses and awareness. This Karan was nothing but your writer of this book KR Goswami who is narrating this story and this book as a whole.

My mental barrier was not broken by my efforts but few people around me and the almighty who saved me to survive as your writer.

The story is not about anybody else but KR Goswami, the author of this narrative. My obstacles were not overcome solely through my endeavors; rather, it was the support of a few individuals around me and the divine intervention that enabled me to endure and continue as your writer.

Thank you!

Conclusion

I have tried to provide a reflective journey, consolidating the profound insights gained throughout this transformative exploration. The path to self-discovery and empowerment has been illuminated, offering a holistic guide for cultivating resilience, mastering mindset, and sustaining unwavering motivation.

My book may serve as the crowning jewel, emphasizing the importance of mindfulness in perpetuating motivation. As discussed throughout the book in detail into the intricate dance between setbacks and progress, the narrative must have weaved a tapestry of resilience, demonstrating that setbacks are not roadblocks but stepping stones toward personal growth.

The power of mindfulness is unraveled, revealing its role as the cornerstone of sustained motivation. By embracing setbacks as integral components of the journey, individuals are empowered to navigate challenges with grace and resilience. I also tried to provide practical strategies for overcoming setbacks, building emotional resilience, and fostering a mindful lifestyle that fuels long-term motivation.

As the final piece of the puzzle, the "Mindful Momentum" was framed to underscore the interconnectedness of all preceding ideas. The inner strength blueprint, adaptive agility, fearless forward movement, and victorious vulnerability converge to create a resilient mindset that withstands the tests of uncertainty and adversity.

I want to encourage you to reflect on your unique journeys and recognize the strength within vulnerability, the transformative power of adapting to change, and the beauty of imperfection. The book can never conclude without your calls to action, urging you to apply the acquired knowledge in your daily lives, fostering a positive and empowering mental attitude.

I truly believe that "Break the Mental Barriers" will stand as a guidebook for those seeking to conquer obstacles, build resilience, and turn setbacks into victories. I conclude that as a final destination but as a launching pad for continued growth, mindful living, and the perpetual pursuit of personal triumphs. I want to leave you with a renewed sense of purpose, armed with the tools and wisdom to face life's challenges with unwavering strength and resilience.